BASIC ILLUSTRATED

Snowshoeing

Eli Burakian

FALCONGUIDES

GUILFORD, CONNECTICUT
HELENA, MONTANA
AN IMPRINT OF GLOBE PEQUOT PRESS

FALCONGUIDES®

FalconGuides is an imprint of Globe Pequot Press.
Falcon, FalconGuides, and Outfit Your Mind are registered trademarks of Morris Book Publishing, LLC.

Photos by Eli Burakian except for the following: pages 44, 48 by Carl Burak; page 65 (bottom) by Jevan Stubits; page 76 © powerofforever/IStock.com; and those licensed by Shutterstock.com: page 61 © Maridav; page 72 © scattoselvaggio; page 88 © fstockfoto

Text design: Karen Williams (intudesign.net)
Project editor: Julie Marsh
Layout: Sue Murray

Library of Congress Cataloging-in-Publication data is available on file.

ISBN 978-0-7627-7765-5

Printed in the United States of America

10 9 8 7 6 5 4 3 2 1

Contents

Acknowledgments

This book would not have been possible without the help from these wonderful people: Julia Burakian, Carl Burak, Sadie Martiesian, Jason Martiesian, Lisa Martiesian, Jennifer Martiesian, Bernardino Ramos, Dorothy Martiesian, Terrance Martiesian, Jevan Stubits, Brian Kunz, Kestrel Kunz, Daniel Wainberg, and Katherine McWalters. I'd also like to thank Kahtoola for providing sample snowshoes.

Introduction

Boy, have you got some fun in store! You are now taking the first steps through a door, beyond which lie infinite possibilities in snow-based enjoyment. Snowshoes, quite simply, make it much more efficient to travel through snow-covered terrain. The winter world is your oyster, and now you have the means to explore nature in locations and environments that may have previously seemed inaccessible.

By no means is snowshoeing easy, however. It takes a lot of work to move through snow, especially in hilly and mountainous terrain. This book does not cover everything that you need to know to travel in the winter, but by learning, practicing, and absorbing the information that lies within, you will be well on your way to boatloads of fun.

I first discovered snowshoeing while living in New Hampshire during college. After exploring the local trails, I began to take my snowshoe adventures farther away from my home. Although I loved backcountry skiing, snowshoes enabled me to move in terrain that was often thick with undergrowth, saplings, rocks, and ice, common impediments in the northeastern United States.

When I finally had the opportunity to create my first book on photography, about Mount Moosilauke, an above tree-line mountain located in the White Mountains of

Snowshoeing is a meaningful family activity. Here, Brian shows daughter Kestral fox tracks in the snow.

New Hampshire, snowshoes became a necessity. The perfect photograph is never in the most accessible spot, and by using small, maneuverable snowshoes, I was able to get myself to snow-covered vantage points, from which few other photographs had ever been taken.

One of the most appealing aspects of snowshoeing is its accessibility. First, snowshoeing is a relatively inexpensive way to enjoy the winter. Skiing requires not only proper winter attire, but also boots, bindings, skis, poles, helmets, and other important pieces of gear. Snowshoeing, at a bare minimum, requires only

There is something truly special about walking up a mountain on a beautiful, sunny midwinter day.

the proper footwear and a pair of snowshoes. (As mentioned later in this book, a pair of hiking poles will make your snowshoe adventures much more enjoyable.) Snowshoes can often be rented as well.

Second, snowshoeing is very easy to learn. There are plenty of tips that will make your snowshoe experience more enjoyable, safe, and efficient, but in essence, snowshoeing is just walking with big paddles on your feet to distribute your weight. If you can walk, you can snowshoe.

Use this book as a reference. You may not find it necessary to read every word verbatim, but by becoming familiar with the content and using the images as references, your introduction to snowshoeing will be relatively painless. Soon you'll be looking at any place covered in snow as prime terrain for your exploring.

Enjoy the book, give snowshoeing a try, have fun, and stay safe!

CHAPTER 1

Choosing Your Snowshoes

Before embarking on any outing, it is important to have the right equipment, and snowshoeing is no different. Snowshoes come in a variety of shapes, sizes, and materials, and choosing the correct snowshoe may mean the difference between a pleasant outdoor adventure or a frustrating time flailing through the snow.

Regardless of what advertisers may tell you, snowshoes are used for one main purpose: to make it easier to walk on snow. If a snowshoe is not making it easier to walk on snow, it is not serving its purpose. Simply, a snowshoe is meant to distribute your weight over a larger surface area, thus decreasing the depth to which your foot sinks. Snowshoes are practical when it would otherwise take too much energy, or would even be unsafe, to travel over snow in regular footwear. Additionally, snowshoes can provide a certain amount of traction when the snow is slippery or there is ice, and they can also help keep your feet dry.

Many factors go into choosing the proper pair of snowshoes. Snow conditions can vary from fresh light powder to heavy slush to wind-crusted snow and even ice. Snow depth plays a big role as well. Will you be traveling on untracked deep snow, or will the path already be completely packed down? Weight also plays an important factor, as the heavier the person, the larger the snowshoe will need

Jump into snowshoeing. You won't regret it!

to be in order to provide an ample amount of flotation. If you plan on carrying a heavy backpack, keep in mind that your total weight will be increased.

Another important factor in choosing a snowshoe is the type of terrain on which the snowshoe will be used. Will you be traveling on flat open ground, moving over hilly rolling terrain, or scaling steep mountains? Less important, but also a factor, is the user's height. A shorter person may prefer shorter snowshoes. Other factors to keep in mind are affordability, ease of use, and durability.

You may be thinking, "Uh oh, I didn't realize it would be so difficult. I don't know where to begin!" Don't worry, though: Many snowshoes will work for a variety of people under a variety of conditions. Yes, there are snowshoes that are tailored perfectly to a particular need, but there are also many that will work perfectly fine as an "all-around" snowshoe. One of the benefits of modern technology is that snowshoes are much more versatile than they used to be.

Anatomy of a Snowshoe

Prior to choosing a snowshoe, it is important to be familiar with all of its parts. We will discuss the different types of snowshoes momentarily, but all snowshoes share these similar parts.

Binding

This is where your foot attaches to the snowshoe. The binding should rotate freely, allowing your toes to move forward through the opening in the snowshoe. It consists of four different parts.

The **plate** is the surface on which your foot rests. In modern snowshoes it is usually metal or plastic, covered by a grippy surface.

The **straps** hold your foot to the snowshoe. The more securely the foot is attached to the snowshoe, the better you are able to control the snowshoe and less energy is wasted. Straps vary in style and material. These include laces on traditional snowshoes and nylon, plastic, or rubber straps on more modern snowshoes, which usually attach via metal or plastic buckles.

There are many types of bindings, so try a few to see what is right for you. This binding features rubber straps, which are easy to use with mittens.

The **cleats and crampons** are sharp spikes that protrude from the bottom of the binding. When present, these are always under the toe and often under the instep. Their purpose is to dig into or grab onto the ground, ice, or packed snow under your feet to prevent slipping. The steeper and more technical the terrain, the more important these become (more on this below).

The **pivot rod** or **pivot strap** is the metal bar or strap where the binding attaches to the snowshoe. Often a pivot rod allows the binding to rotate freely, enabling a fairly large angle between the foot and the snowshoe. This can be ideal for steeper terrain. Pivot straps usually provide less degree of rotation. Although possibly not as ideal on steeper terrain, the lower amount of rotation provided by a pivot strap prevents extra movement with the snowshoe and can make going downhill easier. Some people like the increased control with snowshoe bindings that rotate less, but a downside to be wary of is snow flying up one's back every step on the downhill.

Decking or Webbing

The decking includes most of the surface area of the snowshoe. In traditional wood snowshoes, this is often cowhide or leather lacing in a weave. Today most modern snowshoes use synthetic material that is fairly stiff, yet able to absorb the impact of rocks and debris without breaking. The decking on modern snowshoes is usually fairly solid, without any major holes.

Some modern snowshoes are made of molded plastic. Instead of a separate decking attached to a frame, the entire snowshoe, other than the spikes and binding, is made out of one hard, solid piece of plastic.

Toe

The toe is the front of the snowshoe. Traditional snowshoes are often flat here, but most modern snowshoes have an upturned toe, which allows for the snowshoe to rise out of a depression without digging into the snow in front.

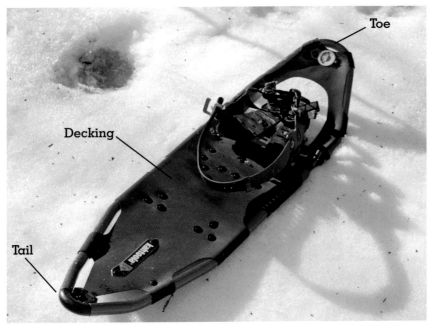

This snowshoe has an upturned toe to prevent digging into the snow. The decking, which is attached to the frame, provides the surface area and thus the flotation.

Tail

The tail of the snowshoe is the section of snowshoe behind the foot. A longer tail helps with straight tracking in open terrain, while a shorter tail is more maneuverable. The tail also provides counterweight to the tip, helping to create a balance from front to back.

Crampons and Traction Bars

The crampons under the toe and the ball of the foot, on the bottom part of the binding, allow the snowshoe to dig into the ground. This may be packed snow or even ice. There are often crampon spikes in the rear of the snowshoe, which also aid in stability. The length, number, and design of these spikes vary depending on the particular purpose of that snowshoe. Some snowshoes also have traction bars running partway along the length of the snowshoe, behind the foot. These traction bars

The cleats or spikes provide traction on slick snow and ice. This snowshoe has spikes under the foot as well as under and behind the heel.

help prevent unwanted slipping from lateral movement. Traditional snowshoes do not usually have traction devices.

Heel Riser

Many modern snowshoes have an object on which your heel rests. This can be rotated vertically to prevent your heel from having to travel all the way back down to the plane of the decking, thus saving a lot of extra movement and wasted energy on steep uphill climbs.

The heel lift/riser prevents the heel from returning all the way back to the decking. This helps save energy on steep uphills.

Sizing

When choosing a snowshoe, it is important that it is the correct size. If the snowshoe is too big, the user will feel awkward and balance could be an issue. On the other side of the coin, if the snowshoe is too small, it may not perform the proper function of preventing the user from sinking too low. A smaller snowshoe has less surface area, and therefore less area to distribute weight.

As mentioned earlier, it is important to factor in the user's entire weight to determine the correct size. For example, if you are going on an overnight hike, you might be carrying a backpack full of camping supplies, such as a tent, sleeping bag, and cooking gear, along with extra food. Additionally, if it is cold, you may be wearing a good amount of clothing, which also adds weight.

There is no easy formula to determine the correct size, as even snowshoes with the same overall surface area may provide different amounts of flotation due to varying geometries and construction methods. Most modern snowshoes are accompanied by a chart that lists the correct size for a specific model based on weight and intended use.

Snowshoes come in many shapes and sizes.

Length of Snowshoes

Longer snowshoes are typically ideal for tracking in one direction, especially when these snowshoes are also narrower. Shorter snowshoes, however, are more maneuverable.

Width of Snowshoes

Generally snowshoes are longer than they are wide. Hence, the wider the snowshoe, the more the weight is distributed around the foot on all sides, which in turn decreases the amount that the snowshoes sink. A wider snowshoe can also be shorter, which allows more maneuverability. A snowshoe is too wide if it prevents a person from walking and standing comfortably in a normal stance.

Bindings

Bindings are usually adjustable and accommodate a number of different sizes. Be sure to try on the binding before purchasing a pair of snowshoes. Also keep in mind that a heavy-duty winter boot will fit differently than a lightweight sneaker, and it is important that the bindings accommodate all of the different footwear that you may use while snowshoeing. The foot must be able to rotate freely through the front opening.

Types of Snowshoes

In the world of snowshoes, function dictates form. As with most outdoor gear these days, you can find snowshoes that fit every specific need. That being said, the advancement of snowshoe design, which incorporates much more durable and lightweight materials than existed even fifteen years ago, has allowed a broadening of the snowshoe categories. You should be able to find a snowshoe that fits most, if not all, of your needs and will work in a variety of conditions, from steep icy terrain, to flat fields covered in deep powder, to rolling packed trails.

Modern snowshoes, and even traditional snowshoes, now incorporate features that can be found in more than one category below, broadening the scope of conditions that the snowshoes can be used in and the type and size of people who use them. Nonetheless, it is important to be aware of the different types of snowshoes available in order to make a wise choice.

Mountaineering

These snowshoes may also be called "backcountry" or "technical." Generally mountaineering snowshoes have been designed for use on steep slopes, rocky and icy terrain, or places with variable conditions where both grip and maneuverability are very important.

Snowshoes in this category are often smaller than those in other categories, giving up flotation for maneuverability. Additionally, mountaineering snowshoes usually have more and longer crampon spikes. These snowshoes can be expensive, as they usually use high-tech, lightweight, and durable materials. They are meant to be used in places where every ounce matters and equipment failure is not an option. Mountaineering snowshoes made with the highest-tech materials, such as carbon fiber, can decrease the overall weight by a few ounces but often add a significant amount of cost.

Recreational

Recreational snowshoes should fill the need of the majority of snowshoe enthusiasts. Very similar to mountaineering snowshoes, these snowshoes are built to work in a variety of conditions. Somewhat less rugged and with smaller traction devices than those found on the mountaineering snowshoes, they are often slightly larger than the mountaineering variety, allowing for more flotation in deeper snow.

This snowshoe is made out of molded plastic and is smaller than many, making it ideal for steeper, more technical ascents. It also is very suitable for recreational use in moderate snow.

Snowshoes falling in this category are usually less expensive than mountaineering snowshoes, but still use materials that are durable and lightweight. By using materials such as aluminum for frames, or molded plastic for the entire decking and frame, these snowshoes can be very light without adding much expense.

Most of the snowshoes that you will find at a modern outdoor retailer will fall into the recreational category.

Sport

Sport snowshoes can also be called "running" or "racing" snowshoes. As these names imply, snowshoes in this category are usually used by people who want to run or at least move very fast, usually on packed terrain. These snowshoes are much smaller than those in either of the previous two categories, allowing them to be lightweight and highly maneuverable. Because snowshoe racers are usually running where other people have gone before, there is no need for large snowshoes with a lot of surface area.

Although most snowshoes have a right and left foot, often the only distinction between the two is the side on which the lacing or buckles of the binding attach. Sport snowshoes, however, are often asymmetrical, with the shape of each snowshoe specifically designed to be worn on a particular side.

These snowshoes generally are not great in a variety of conditions and are really geared to people whose main concern is moving quickly.

Traditional

For the sake of this book, I am referring to a traditional snowshoe as any snowshoe that is made out of wood and other natural materials. Snowshoes of this type were originally developed by Native Americans and were used to allow efficient travel over snow-covered terrain, a necessity for hunting and food gathering in the harsh winter months.

The frames of these snowshoes are made out of wood. The decking, or webbing, is usually made out of hide or leather, woven in a pattern that is tight enough to provide flotation but still has open holes to keep the weight reasonable and the snowshoe repairable. Due to the fact

Traditional snowshoes are great for flotation when the snow is deep. Here is a bearpaw-type snowshoe with modern strap bindings.

that these snowshoes are not as light and do not have solid decking, they are often larger than comparable modern snowshoes that provide the same amount of flotation.

Although not as well-suited for steeper, icier terrain due to the lack of any significant traction devices, these snowshoes may still be ideal for many people. Manufacturers still making these snowshoes have incorporated modern engineering technology with newer shapes and modern bindings.

Before eschewing traditional snowshoes, keep in mind that they are often less expensive than modern types. Additionally, because they are made out of wood, they have a slight amount of flexibility, which can be nice in undulating terrain and can provide the wearer with more "feel." Snowshoes of this type also have a storied history and a beauty that is unmatched by modern snowshoes.

Traditional snowshoes can be perfect for very deep snow, but have very little traction if the going gets slippery. Though there are many variations, traditional snowshoes generally fall under the following main styles.

The **pickerel** is very long and narrow, allowing for travel in open terrain on dry snow. Originally developed by people in the arctic or subarctic regions, where tight trees were not an issue, these snowshoes are fast but not very maneuverable,

The **Maine or Michigan** snowshoe is also fairly long and is wider than the pickerel. These snowshoes are also good for deep snow and are characterized by long narrow tails, which help them track in one direction. Like the pickerel, these snowshoes are not ideal for places where maneuverability is important.

The **bearpaw** is an oval, almost round, snowshoe that gives up flotation for maneuverability. Modified bearpaws are similar but have a narrower heel and an upturned toe, allowing for smoother travel on the descents.

The **western or Green Mountain** snowshoe is a longer, narrower version of the traditional bearpaw. These snowshoes are oval shaped, have upturned toes, and are the basis for modern snowshoe design.

Traditional snowshoes are made in shapes and sizes that best suit the environment in which they will be used. The snowshoe on the right also makes great waffles.

Hybrid or Specialized

This is a bit of a "catch-all" category. The advent of a larger consumer base, new technologies, and new materials has allowed snowshoe manufacturers to create products that meet the needs of a broad array of users. You can now find snowshoes that are specifically engineered for children, snowshoes that are expandable for different snow types or varying weight, and even snowshoes that have removable bindings.

Snowshoes for children are often made of molded plastic. They are much smaller and much less expensive than snowshoes for adults.

MSR (Mountain Safety Research) offers snowshoes that are expandable. Extra tail pieces can be purchased separately and attached to the snowshoes, allowing for flexibility. Add on the tail piece if you are carrying a lot of weight or the snowshoes are going to be used by someone who is heavy.

Kahtoola makes snowshoes that have removable bindings. This serves two functions: First, bindings can be purchased in different sizes,

These snowshoes by MSR allow the attachment of separate tail pieces, thus increasing the total surface area to provide better flotation in deep snow. Here you can see the snowshoes with and without the tail piece.

Checklist: Things to Think About
When Choosing a Snowshoe

When choosing a snowshoe, a number of factors come into play. No snowshoe is perfect for every circumstance, so it is important to choose a snowshoe that fulfills your needs for the places and conditions that will be most often encountered.

Terrain: Will you be traveling on flat ground, hilly ground, or steep mountains? Will you need to be maneuverable in the trees, or will you be traversing open ground?

Snow type and depth: Will you be using the snowshoes on packed trails, deep snow, or icy mixed conditions? Is the snow dry and light or wet and heavy? Drier and lighter snow supports less weight than wet and heavy snow. In the Northwest, Sierra Nevada, and Northeast, you are more likely to encounter denser wet snow. If you're looking for the lightest snow on Earth, look no farther than the Wasatch Mountains in Utah.

Weight of person/people: Are you buying a pair of snowshoes for use by multiple people of different sizes or just for yourself? Make sure to buy snowshoes that can support the weight of the heaviest person expected to regularly use them. Keep in mind the total weight, including gear and clothing, when choosing the right snowshoe.

Cost: Snowshoes vary widely in price. Midrange snowshoes should fill the needs of most consumers. Higher-end snowshoes tend to cost more due to the use of more advanced lightweight materials.

Ease of use: How easy are the snowshoes to put on? You don't want to be out in the woods, freezing your butt off while struggling to put your snowshoes back on. Some types of straps are also easier to put on with gloves or even mittens. Keep this in mind when assessing a snowshoe purchase, and practice putting on and taking off the snowshoes prior to purchase.

Kahtoola makes a snowshoe that allows the user to remove the binding to be used as a separate crampon. This is ideal in situations where grip and maneuverability are paramount and flotation is not important.

allowing people with small feet and people with big feet to use the same snowshoes. Second, the bindings themselves become crampons, providing traction and maneuverability when traction is important and flotation is not.

There are many other types of interesting designs, and more are being developed every year.

Beyond Snowshoes: Other Important Gear

Whether you plan on going out for an hour or a few days, an enjoyable snowshoeing adventure requires having appropriate gear. When snowshoeing in the winter, it is important that your footwear and clothing keep you warm and dry. The ability to easily adjust to changing conditions is necessary not only for comfort, but also for safety.

You may think that snowshoeing is only a winter sport, but actually some of my most enjoyable snowshoeing outings have taken place in the summer. Mountains and locations that receive large snowfall throughout the winter often have a huge snowpack lasting well into the summer. In fact, snowshoeing in the spring and summer allows you to enjoy the extended daylight, providing the opportunity for longer single-day outings.

Regardless of when or where you snowshoe, having the right gear is essential. Carrying too much gear will be uncomfortable, but not having the right footwear or clothing when needed can turn a short, enjoyable day trip into a miserable experience. Proper eyewear is crucial when traveling on snow, especially when it is sunny, and using poles can allow you to travel faster and safer over different types of terrain.

Poles

As Leki, a major pole manufacturer, has stated in its advertising, "Four legs are better than two!" Nowhere is this statement truer than when traveling in snow. Poles provide innumerable benefits and will guarantee a more enjoyable experience.

All Poles Are Not Created Equal

Maybe you found an old pair of poles in the basement. Certainly any poles are better than none. The ideal poles, however, are **collapsible.** This allows two advantages: First, they can be adjusted in length depending on the type of terrain encountered or the user's height.

Second, they collapse small enough to fit in your backpack or at least be strapped onto the outside without getting in your way when you don't need them. It also makes it easier to travel, as collapsed poles can fit in most luggage. Some poles adjust using locking latches while others use a twist mechanism (right is tight, left is loose). Some poles have two sections and others have three, allowing them to collapse even smaller.

Poles are generally made out of lightweight metal such as aluminum. Some high-tech poles are composed of carbon fiber, but in most circumstances metal poles are better. They can

The locking mechanism on this pole allows it to adjust in size, which is ideal for traveling over variable terrain. This also allows for adjustment to the user's height and provides easier storage in a backpack or bag.

Wrist straps allow for a relaxed grip, and a big winter basket above the tip prevents the pole from plunging deep into the snow.

bend but usually will not break, which is ideal if you fall or the pole gets stuck somewhere.

Many modern poles also contain **springs,** which aid in the absorption of shock, allowing for a more comfortable descent. Some of these can be adjusted from no spring to a large amount. Poles with springs are usually more expensive and add one more working part that can fail in the field. They are certainly not necessary, especially while snowshoeing, since the snow acts as a natural shock absorber.

Other parts of the pole include the basket, grip, strap, and tip. The **basket** prevents the pole from jabbing straight through the snow. Generally larger baskets are used in the winter, especially when the snow is light and deep. Unless there is very little snow, large baskets are a necessity. If the pole you are using does not have large baskets, you can find replacement winter baskets at most outdoor gear shops or ski shops.

The **grip** is a matter of preference. Some grips are plastic, others are cork, and many are rubber. Some angle forward to allow the pole tip to be planted in a more effective position. Make sure the grip is comfortable, both with and without gloves on.

The **strap** is what holds the pole to your hand. Make sure the straps are easy to adjust and they fit your hands with gloves on.

The **tip** on less expensive poles is just an extension of the metal shaft, tapering down to a point. Most modern collapsible poles, however, have replaceable tips, which is nice if the tip snaps or gets bent. On any long trip I'll bring along an extra tip, just in case. The point of the tip can be the same metal as the pole, rubber, or even a special type of metal to grab onto rocks or ice. A metal tip can help your pole dig in if you are traveling over ice or compacted snow.

Why Use Poles?

Poles will aid your snowshoe adventure in a number of ways. They come in handy when you need to have another stable platform for balancing. The adage of "three points of contact" is a good one to follow whenever you are in a position where stability is paramount. Whether climbing over a log, crossing a stream, or even traversing across uneven or slanted terrain, poles can provide that extra level of support allowing you to move confidently over impediments.

By using poles you can also give your legs a little bit of a break. Pushing against the poles while traveling over flat terrain or going uphill allows your arms and upper body to aid in your forward momentum. I also like using poles because they give my arms and upper body something to do and make the outing a full-body experience. If you are going to bring your arms with you, why not use them?

One of the main benefits of using poles is their ability to absorb some of your weight when moving downhill. They can greatly reduce the amount of work your knees have to do and can even prevent injury. Forcing your knees to absorb the entire weight of your body and everything you are carrying, especially while moving down a steep slope, is a recipe for knee injury.

On the down side, poles can be impractical in some situations when the hands are needed for other purposes, such as when hunting or carrying a load.

Sizing and Attaching Poles

Using poles is not rocket science, but a few tips can help you get moving quickly and efficiently.

First, adjust the length of your poles to one that feels comfortable. Every person will have an individual preference, but a good rule of thumb is to have the tops of the poles extend 4 to 6 inches above your waist. When measuring keep in mind that the snow will compact under

Slide your hand up through the strap, then hold onto the strap and the grip. The pole should be able to swing freely in a nice loose grasp.

the basket of the pole, so make sure to measure from the point where the pole no longer sinks, or when it touches the hard ground.

Believe it or not, properly attaching the pole to your wrist will allow you to use the poles much more efficiently. Remove any twists in the strap, and open it to create an O. Now, put your hand up through the bottom of the O and grip the pole. The strap should sit in the crook between your thumb and index finger, with it resting against the inside of your hand. Adjust the length of the strap so that when you are loosely gripping the pole, the back of the strap is sitting comfortably on the back of your hand near your wrist.

Attaching the strap in this manner allows a number of benefits over just sticking your hand in from the top and grabbing. The pole will be able to swing freely on your wrist, allowing you to have a much looser, relaxed grip on the pole while it swings freely with your movements. It also gives you another leverage point, as you can push against the strap as well as grip the handle. You will also be able to grip the top

One of the best uses for poles is as a glove rack. Just put your gloves on the grips while you use your camera or get some food.

of the pole easily, as I like to do when descending steep terrain. If you need to use your hands, say to grab a hold or use your camera, the pole can dangle freely from your wrist.

Snowshoeing with Poles

Now it's time to go! Generally the most comfortable gait involves placing the pole in front on the opposite side of your front foot. So if you are stepping forward with your left foot, you will plant your right pole out in front. Exactly how far in front is a matter of preference and terrain, but generally on flat terrain you'll place it slightly ahead of your front toe. When going uphill the pole will be placed closer to your body, and when going down it will be farther out in front of you.

Make sure to allow the poles to swing freely, as there is no need to grip them tightly. Many people find that adjusting the poles to be shorter when going uphill and longer when going down allows them to keep a nice even gait.

Do not be afraid to adjust the poles while you are snowshoeing until you find a length that works well for you.

Poles aid in balance and allow you to use your upper body during your snowshoe outing. They can also be very helpful on the downhills.

On Your Feet

The two most important aspects to consider when choosing footwear are **comfort** and **moisture control.** Temperature, terrain, and snow type also affect what type of footwear should be used. Although I wish it were the case, snowshoes, however good, will not allow you to float over the snow. Unless the snow is completely packed down, and often even when it is, your shoes will come in contact with the snow.

Boots or Shoes

Regardless of the type of footwear you choose, the first and most important factor is fit. If it is too loose, the extra movement will rub your feet and will more likely cause blisters, and if it's too tight, the point of contact may also create blisters. Depending on temperature and the length of time you will be on your feet, they may also change in size, so footwear with adjustments allow you to tighten or loosen the fit as necessary. Be sure to factor in the type of sock you will be wearing as well, as thicker socks can take up significantly more room than thinner ones.

Footbeds are great for people with flat feet. These molded insoles provide support and can help prevent knee discomfort as well. They range in price from ten or twenty dollars to hundreds of dollars for totally custom orthotics. Off-the-rack brands such as Superfeet or Sof Sole provide the necessary support for most people. If you plan on using footbeds, make sure to put them in before trying on any new footwear.

Footbeds can provide cushion and/or support. They range from foam pads to custom-molded orthotics.

Unless you are snowshoeing in extremely warm weather and will be out for only a short while, your footwear will need to be either **water-resistant** or **waterproof.** Moisture is your enemy, and wet feet create friction that causes blisters and other foot irritations. Water-resistant footwear tends to allow feet to "breathe," enabling moisture to escape. Believe it or not, in conditions where it is comfortable but still cold enough to prevent the snow from melting, water-resistant boots will keep your feet drier than waterproof boots, which in addition to preventing moisture from entering can also prevent it from escaping.

That being said, fabrics such as Gore-Tex claim to be waterproof while allowing breathability. Experience suggests this is somewhat accurate. True waterproof boots are usually made with leather, rubber, or some type of nonporous synthetic material and are ideal when the temperature is near or above freezing, the snow is wet and heavy, or there is any open water. Most heavy-duty winter boots are waterproof, as the non-breathability allows them to retain heat.

Depending upon the temperature and snowpack, you may want a heavy winter boot, a midweight hiking boot, or a light trail runner.

Only when it is really cold, and you think your feet may get cold, is an insulated boot ideal. Boots for cold temperatures often have a temperature rating. Keep in mind that if it's too cold, you probably won't be out snowshoeing.

In many conditions a mid- to high-top midweight hiking boot can be ideal in winter. The added support afforded by a higher-ankle boot can help prevent injury. A heavy insulated boot generally will work well when it is really cold, but will leave your feet sweaty in warmer conditions. A midweight hiking boot made from synthetics and/or leather should allow enough room for you to add heavier socks if it gets very cold. Shoes or boots that reach higher up the ankle will prevent snow from getting in your footwear, but once the snow is fairly deep, gaiters and/or snow pants are the only surefire way to keep snow out.

Mukluks are smooth-bottomed hide and canvas footwear that can easily slip into and out of traditional single-strap bindings. The design has remained the same for many years, and modern mukluk makers are adding tread on the bottom to allow for more varied uses.

Still popular today when using traditional snowshoes, mukluks are boots made of leather (such as moose hide) and canvas. With simple traditional bindings, mukluks can allow quick and easy putting on and taking off of the snowshoes.

> ### Checklist: Footwear on the Mind
> **Temperature:** Is it warm, cold, or frigid? Will your feet breathe, or will they need insulation to keep them warm?
>
> **Snow type:** If it is well below freezing, it's unlikely the snow will melt and your feet will stay dry, but if the snow is wet and heavy, make sure your footwear can keep them dry.
>
> **Laces:** Certain types of laces seem to work better at staying tied when wet or freezing. Make sure that you can still untie your laces if they get wet and frozen.
>
> **Waterproofing:** Waterproof boots, including leather boots, repel moisture much better after liquid or spray waterproofing is applied to the surface. This is especially true when the boots are no longer new. Many types of waterproofing products are available at shoe and gear stores.
>
> **Weight:** When a heavy boot is not necessary, opt for a lighter shoe. The weight on your feet is not insignificant, and you will use much less energy wearing footwear that does not weigh a ton.

Socks

Having the proper socks is just as important as having the proper boot or shoe. Everybody has individual preferences with socks, but one thing I cannot emphasize enough is **do not wear cotton socks!** Once wet, cotton socks will create a lot of friction, almost guaranteeing blisters. Additionally, wet cotton socks provide no insulating value, so if it is cold, your feet will freeze.

Until recently most winter hikers used lightweight silk or synthetic liners under heavy ragg wool socks. These days there are many amazing different types of socks, and liners are no longer necessary. Some of the most popular and comfortable socks on the market are comprised of a wool-synthetic blend. Wool is a

Wool socks or wool/synthetic blends are ideal for snowshoeing, as they insulate even when wet and will help prevent chafing. Do not wear cotton socks.

great insulator, even when wet, and synthetic materials allow the socks to stretch evenly, dry quickly, and breathe well. Popular brands include SmartWool and Thorlos, but there are countless others to choose from. (Personally, I love Darn Tough socks, made in my home state of Vermont. They include a lifetime guarantee.) Some all-wool socks are comfortable as well, and the new entirely synthetic socks can also provide a good mixture of weight, comfort, and insulation.

When choosing socks, make sure there are no seams that may irritate your foot. Pick socks that come above the ankle of your shoes or boots. Make sure the socks fit nicely on your feet, inside your shoes or boots. High-performance socks come in a variety of weights. Thin socks work great in warm conditions and can dry quickly. Thick socks add a lot of insulating value but in warmer conditions can leave your feet wet and sweaty.

Choose socks that fit well and are warm enough but not too thick. I usually carry at least one extra pair of socks when I snowshoe, as I can double up if it gets really cold or change them out if they get wet.

Gaiters

Gaiters are fabric coverings that go over the ankle and the boot or shoe opening. They are the key to keeping your feet dry when traveling through snow. Some gaiters are very lightweight and just cinch at the ankle to keep out snow and dust. Others are made of water-resistant or waterproof material, often a breathable version of one of these. They range in length from 6 inches to over a foot.

Winter or waterproof gaiters are usually fairly long, with Velcro on two sides. The gaiter wraps

Gaiters cover boot cuffs to prevent snow from entering and getting your feet wet.

around the ankle, enclosing the top of the boot. Usually a little hook on the bottom of the gaiter attaches to a low shoelace, while a strap goes under the foot from one side to the other, preventing the gaiter from moving up. The strap, the Velcro, and a cinch at the top are adjustable, allowing for good fit and for venting when your feet get too warm.

Some snow pants have gaiters built in, but if you plan on snowshoeing on slushy or deep snow, real gaiters will keep your feet dry. They provide the extra benefit of adding some warmth on cold days and preventing rocks or sand from getting inside the boot.

Clothing

Snowshoeing can be fun in all conditions. The key to enjoying this activity, even in inclement weather, is to be prepared and dressed well. Dressing well involves **layering.** Instead of wearing a heavy jacket and T-shirt, for example, wear a number of lighter layers. These can easily be removed or added, adapting to either the changing outside temperature or a change in body temperature.

Once moving you will be surprised how quickly you warm up. Be sure to take off a layer before getting sweaty, as soaking your clothing early on is a surefire way to get cold later. When you do stop for a break, if it is longer than a minute or two, put on extra layers to prevent your body from cooling down too quickly.

I cannot stress this enough, **do not wear cotton.** Yes, cotton breathes, but once wet it stays wet. Wet clothing is more likely to cause rubbing or friction issues, adds weight, and most important, sucks vital heat from your body once you stop moving.

Inner Layer (aka Long Underwear)

The inner layer is the layer against your skin. Since it is very unlikely that this layer will come off at all during your adventure, it is vital to ensure that it is comfortable and breathable, wicking the moisture away from your body. Some people prefer a tight-fitting inner layer, while others prefer a relaxed fit. This layer usually consists of full-length tights or leggings and a long-sleeved shirt.

When it's cold an inner layer of synthetic or wool long underwear will insulate while still providing breathability.

In a modern outdoor or clothing store, you will likely find an astounding assortment of options, ranging from lightweight to heavy and from cheap polyester to fancy high-tech synthetics to wool blends or even straight wool. The synthetics dry quickly and do a good job of wicking moisture, but wool is a good insulator even when wet. The higher-tech fabrics, like Patagonia's Capilene, are truly amazing, but even a cheap polyester top will work better than cotton. One important thing to note, especially if you plan on being around other people before you change, is that wool smells fine even after heavy use, while synthetic clothing seems to start stinking very quickly and can be surprisingly stubborn in returning to a state that will not cause relationship issues.

Some folks still like to wear underwear under this layer. That is fine, but again, make sure it is synthetic, breathable, and doesn't bunch up, creating areas of friction.

A nice layer between your shell and long underwear is a midweight fleece, but anything light and breathable will work.

Middle Layer

The middle layer refers to any and all layers that lie between the inner layer and the outer layer and is often called the "insulating layer." In cold weather you may have quite a number of these, while in very warm weather this layer may be entirely absent. This layer may consist of any of the following: additional synthetic or wool long underwear, a fleece jacket or vest, or a down vest or sweater, to name just a few.

Try different combinations to see what works best for you. Clothing that zippers down the front allows you to remove the layer without having to pull it over your head. This can be nice if you do not want to remove your hat or sunglasses/goggles. A vest can keep your core area warm while allowing your arms to move freely, and layers with zippers or buttons can vent. Venting is a good method to use when you want to release some heat but do not want to remove an entire layer.

A good rule of thumb is to always bring at least one more layer than you think you may need, in case a piece of clothing gets soaked or the weather rapidly deteriorates.

Outer Top Layer (aka Shell)

Choices for this layer run the gamut, and there is no need to get bogged down in all the details. The most important thing to remember when deciding on an outer layer is that this is the piece of clothing that will be exposed to the elements. It may be dry and warm, but if you fall into wet snow, will you stay dry and warm?

Some of the many factors to consider when deciding on an outer layer are warmth, wind resistance, water resistance, and venting capability. If it is cold, make sure that this layer is large enough to fit a number of layers underneath it. When it is really cold, nothing beats goose down for a weight-to-warmth ratio, although synthetic insulation is rapidly catching up and, unlike down, still insulates when it gets wet. Many down jackets are made of breathable water-resistant material and will stay dry even when exposed to a little moisture.

Waterproof and windproof outer layers will keep you warm and dry in winter. Thanks for modeling, Dad!

Jackets with hoods are nice, especially if the weather changes dramatically for the worse. Some jackets also have armpit zipper vents, which do a surprisingly good job at venting extra heat. Unless you are sure you will not overheat, a shell with no insulation and extra middle layers usually functions well. A thick insulated jacket can be great for a short stroll, but if you get hot, it is much less convenient to store in a backpack.

Outer Bottom Layer

This bottom layer can range from thin wind- and water-resistant shell pants to thick waterproof snow pants. Many bottom shells and snow pants have side zippers that allow for venting. Full-length zippers give you the ability to remove the pants without having to take your boots off. You should wear pants that allow your legs to move freely and extend to cover the tops of your boots. Some winter pants also have built-in gaiters.

Make sure the pants are waterproof or highly water-resistant if you plan on sitting or kneeling on the snow at any time. Don't forget to consider ease-of-use when heeding nature's call.

Head and Hands

When your body gets cold, it starts shunting heat from the extremities back to warm the core. This is why as you begin to get cold, your fingers and toes are often the first parts of your body that you'll notice becoming uncomfortable. Wearing a hat can make a huge difference in comfort and is one of the most important elements in temperature regulation.

Gloves or Mittens

As with all the clothing mentioned, gloves range from lightweight to heavy and insulated. You may be comfortable with a midweight pair of winter gloves, but generally it is good to layer here as well. Lightweight synthetic or wool glove liners is a great base layer that provides warmth. These liners come in handy when dexterity is needed but you don't want to expose your bare fingers to the elements. Sometimes it's just really tough to unwrap that Snickers bar with big ol' gloves!

Mittens are usually warmer than gloves because they keep all your fingers together. The tradeoff is dexterity.

This is even truer when wearing mittens. Instead of individually insulating each finger, mittens keep all your fingers together. What you lose in dexterity, you gain in warmth.

A nice feature to look for in gloves and mittens is the wrist strap, which keeps them attached to your wrists even when they're off. It is a shame when you go to get something from your backpack and realize you dropped your glove in the snow!

Hats

Hats vary in size and thickness. I often bring two hats with me in the winter, a thick hat and a thin hat or baseball cap. Choose a hat that is comfortable, and remember to take it off if you feel your head getting hot: A wet hat leads to a cold head. If your hat gets wet with sweat, swap it for your dry hat when you stop.

Hats with brims can help shield your eyes from the sun, which can be overwhelming on clear days on a snow-covered landscape. Full-brimmed hats can also protect the back of your neck from the sun.

Since hats are small and light, it really doesn't make much sense not to carry at least one extra.

Eyewear

If you have ever been out in the snow on a sunny day, you understand the importance of eyewear. Proper eye protection is no joke. Snow blindness, which is more likely to occur at higher elevations, is caused by exposing the eyes in very bright conditions. Symptoms can be so severe that hours after exposure the eyes can get covered in painful blisters and temporary blindness can set in. This is an

Winter hats are remarkable insulators. When it's sunny, snow can be exceptionally bright, so always bring a pair of sunglasses.

extreme example, but any protracted unprotected exposure can lead to headaches and even sunburn on the eyes. In fact, so much light is reflected back from snow that even on cloudy days it is important to wear sunglasses or goggles.

When choosing sunglasses, keep in mind that darker lenses are ideal in bright conditions. High-contrast lenses (orange or yellow) are good in lower light and can make it easier to see in whiteout conditions. Wraparound sunglasses or "glacier" glasses with coverage on the sides prevent extra light from entering in from the side. Polarized glasses are not necessary but can make colors stand out, such as increasing the deep blue of the sky, and can get rid of glare. Many new sunglasses from companies such as Native, Oakley, and Smith allow you to swap in different lenses depending on the conditions.

Goggles have large lenses with frames that sit snug against your skin and a strap that wraps around your head. As with the sunglasses, there are innumerable styles, shapes, colors, and shades. Some goggles provide double lenses or interesting technologies to prevent fogging. Goggles are also ideal when it is windy or very cold, as they provide more protection than sunglasses.

Balaclavas, Neck Warmers, Scarves, and Face Masks

A balaclava is usually made from fleece or similar synthetic material. This article of outerwear goes over your head and wraps around the

front, covering your neck and face and leaving just an opening for goggles.

Neck warmers are also usually made from fleece and are simply tubes that pull over the head and cover the neck. They can be pulled up to protect the lower part of the face as well. Scarves can serve a similar function.

A balaclava can help keep your face, head, and neck warm on very cold days.

Face masks usually are made from neoprene and cinch in the back with Velcro. They have holes for the nose and mouth but cover the rest of the face below the eyes.

These are all small, lightweight accessories that can provide a lot of warmth. When it is really cold, you'll want to limit skin exposure, even on your face.

Backpacks

There are hundreds of styles and sizes of backpacks from which to choose these days. I won't go into detail here, but a few important aspects should be considered when choosing what backpack to bring.

Look for a backpack that has a waterproof, or at least a thick, bottom. Inevitably you will set the pack down in the snow, and it is important that the gear inside stays dry. You can always line the backpack with a plastic bag to ensure the contents do not get wet. Some people prefer a backpack that has holders for water, while others like backpacks that have an integrated water bladder. If it is below freezing, try to keep your water close to your back and insulated so that it will not freeze.

A backpack should be able to fit all of your gear and still have a little room to spare. You may choose to carry additional layers, safety gear, a camera, or extra food and water. Backpacks designed to carry more weight are called "frame packs" and have either an internal or

Choose a backpack that will comfortably fit all your necessary gear, but remember, the heavier your pack, the harder you will need to work. So be prudent with your packing.

external frame as well as a waist belt that function together to transfer much of the weight off your shoulders and onto your hips and legs.

When filling your pack, make sure to leave the items you may want readily available, such as hats, gloves, sunglasses, lip balm, water, and snacks, near the top or in an accessible pouch. You don't want to realize that your gloves are at the bottom, forcing you to go through everything in the pack in order to retrieve them.

Other Gear

As with any outdoor endeavor, you may have personal gear that you always bring along. Keep in mind that the more gear you bring, the heavier your pack will be. Snowshoeing with a heavy pack requires more energy, so it is important to weigh the costs and benefits of bringing extra gear. Some other gear may include:

- **First-aid gear:** Determine what the most likely injuries may be, and prepare for those. Items in a snowshoeing first-aid kit may include, but are not limited to, compression wraps, Band-Aids and bandages, pain relievers, burn cream, chemical hand-warmers, tape, emergency blanket, mirror, and needle and thread.

- **Sunscreen and lip balm:** One can get sunburned even on cloudy days, and sunny days can be extremely dangerous if you are not careful. Be sure to coat all exposed skin every few hours. As the sun reflects off the snow, parts that don't see much sun, like your chin and the bottom of your nose, are likely to get burned. Protect your lips with a lip balm that

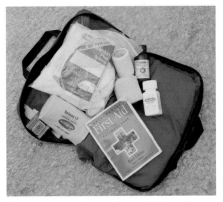

The contents of your first-aid kit will vary depending on the location and conditions of your snowshoe adventure, as well as how long you will be out.

includes sunscreen. (If you become addicted to ChapStick, contact LipBalmAnonymous.com.)

- **Repair kit and duct tape:** If your equipment fails while snowshoeing, the consequences can be much more severe than during a normal summer hike. Bring extra string or rope as well as anything else that may aid in repairing gear in the backcountry. Duct tape is something nobody should travel without. In fact, if you don't have duct tape, put down this book and go get some . . . now.

- **Pack cover:** If it rains or you drop your pack in snow or water, the contents can get wet. Bring along a pack cover to shield your bag from the elements or at least some trash bags with which you can line the inside of your pack.

- **GPS and/or compass:** It is not only important to carry a GPS and/or compass, but also vital you know how to use it. If you get lost, which can happen to the best of us, it is most likely to happen in snowy whiteout conditions or in the dark. Know how to use your GPS or compass, in combination with a map, to find your way. If you are returning to the same place from where you departed, you can mark a waypoint to find your way back.

- **Maps and guidebooks:** Use common sense and don't travel in unfamiliar terrain without adequate materials to find your way. Know how to read a map and refer to it throughout the trip. Maps can also show you where important features are, such as lakes, ponds, rivers, and streams. Maps printed on Tyvek or similar material are much better for winter travel, as paper maps will fall apart when wet. Keep paper maps in a clear plastic ziplock bag, with the relevant side displayed.

- **Food and water:** Did I really need to list this here? Humans need food to survive. You are a human. Bring food that you will enjoy and that will supply energy. The easier it is to eat with gloves on, the more likely you will be to eat it. Keep water in a tight container, and if it's well below freezing, make sure it is insulated enough to stay liquid. Snowshoeing in the winter affords the opportunity to bring food such as sandwiches, meat, fruit, and vegetables that would not fare well in warmer environments. Keep food cold by making sure it is not lying against your body.

- **Stove:** If you are out for multiple days or will be traveling a long enough distance to need more water than you can carry, make sure you bring and know how to use a stove. If it's below freezing, the only way to get water may be to melt snow or ice, so make sure you have enough fuel to melt what you need. There are many canister stoves that are lightweight and very simple to use. White gas stoves, which are a little more complicated, do better in colder conditions.

If you plan on being out for a while and the temperature is well below freezing, a stove will allow you to melt snow for water. A white gas stove like this is better than a canister stove when it's very cold.

- **Cell phone:** If you are in an area with coverage, bring a cell phone with you—it can be a lifesaver if you find yourself in serious trouble. Keep it close to your body to keep the battery warm, and bring an extra battery if possible. Know that when you are out of cell phone range, you will have no ability to contact a rescue party. Many cell phones, such as Apple's iPhone, can also double as a GPS, video camera, and still camera, among other things.

- **Knife or multitool:** A Leatherman, Swiss army knife, or other multitool can help in many situations, including repairs or cutting the salami and cheese. There is no need to carry a large knife, as a small one can usually serve all purposes.

- **Headlamp or flashlight:** If you get caught out after dark, a headlamp or flashlight can be a lifesaver. Make sure the batteries are fresh. Headlamps are nice, as they allow you to maintain the use of both hands. New LED lights are bright and lightweight, and the batteries last for a very long time.

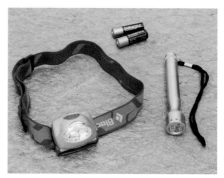

Always bring a headlamp or flashlight with you, even if you plan on returning before dark.

- **Matches or lighter:** Better safe than sorry! If you need to light a fire, better have something to start it with.

- **Waterproof stuff sacks or plastic bags:** Make sure you have enough bags to keep all your gear dry. If you don't want to buy waterproof stuff sacks, Baggies or plastic trash bags work well. Ziplock bags are great for smaller items like papers and maps that need to stay dry and visible.

By putting your various gear in plastic bags, you can make sure it stays dry and organized.

- **Plastic ground sheet:** If the terrain is covered in snow, a plastic sheet can provide a dry spot to sit down for a rest or have lunch.

- **Toilet paper:** Don't forget the TP, or you may be s**t out of luck! Pack out, bury, or burn your used paper. Check on the specific rules for the area you will be visiting.

- **Sleeping bag and pad:** If you plan on staying out overnight, make sure to have a mummy-shaped sleeping bag and a thick pad to insulate you from the snow. Foam and inflatable pads can also be nice for sitting down on the snow and can come in handy even for a day hike.

- **Tent:** If you plan on sleeping out overnight, a tent not only provides shelter from the elements, but also can keep you much warmer as your body heat warms the inside area and you are not exposed to the wind.

- **Camera:** Show your friends and family your adventure. Many companies make great compact cameras that are both waterproof and shock resistant. Bring extra batteries, as they fare poorly in cold conditions.

- **Change of clothes:** If you will be spending the night or will be out for a while, be sure to carry comfortable dry clothes so you won't be stuck in your wet hiking gear, and set aside dry clothes to change into at the end of the hike.

- **Other personal gear:** Obviously this is just a list of suggestions. If you wear contact lenses or glasses, have specific health requirements, or anything else, use your judgment to determine the necessity of bringing more personal gear. That being said, heavy packs suck, so bring only what you need!

CHAPTER 3

Basic Snowshoeing Technique

In its most basic essence, snowshoeing is just walking on snow. If you can walk, you can snowshoe. Snowshoeing should be a source of enjoyment, a way to appreciate nature during times of year that are unique. A short stroll or vigorous extended exercise, it's your choice!

There is no doubt that if you grabbed a pair of snowshoes, put them on correctly, and headed out the door, it would not take very long to become comfortable. Right, left, right, left . . . you get the idea. Within an hour you most likely will have figured out many of the tips and tricks that make snowshoeing more efficient. And that's really the goal: conserve energy for moving farther, faster, or just getting a chance to take a look around. Less work equals bigger smiles.

A few simple steps, and you'll be snowshoeing in no time!

The techniques discussed in this chapter are not rocket science. But having an idea of these energy-saving tips will give you an understanding of how best to approach the sport.

Putting on Your Snowshoes

There are many different types of bindings. Make sure that you understand how to work the strap system and that everything is in working order before you head out the door. The best way to ruin a trip is to find out something is wrong only after hitting the trail.

The easiest way to put on snowshoes is by **sitting down,** either in a chair or on a log, or by **kneeling.** Standing upright then bending fully at the waist with both feet under you is a surefire way to start your trip with a head rush. If kneeling, put one knee behind you on the ground and the other foot out in front, where you can easily access the straps.

When fastening the straps to your feet, be sure to cinch them tightly enough to get rid of any extra play. Extra movement wastes energy. Don't cinch them so tightly that you cut off any circulation, however, as this may cause your toes to get cold.

By kneeling down when strapping on your snowshoes you can prevent the full-bend head rush.

When standing up, move a leg forward to push off from. You can use the poles to push against, either on the ground or planted in the snow. If you plant your pole in the snow, be careful not to grab the pole above the level of your shoulder, as this can put a lot of strain on the shoulder joint.

To **stand up,** get in the aforementioned kneeling position with one leg forward, and with the help of your arms pushing against your poles, use your front leg to push you up.

First Steps

Golf courses are great places to get comfortable walking in snowshoes, as they provide flat ground and usually a few hills as well. Regardless, find a nice, open, flat spot. Keep in mind that deep snow makes snowshoeing much more difficult, so you may want to embark on this adventure in a place where there is moderate snow (less than 10 inches of soft snow) or there is a packed trail.

Going Straight

Ideally your snowshoes are narrow enough to allow you to maintain a normal stance. You may have to widen your stance slightly, so don't be surprised if your hip flexors are a little sore after your first day. As you walk forward, remember to lift your leg high enough to clear the snow ahead, but no higher. If you find you are stepping on your snowshoes from behind, lengthen your stride a little bit.

While stepping forward, plant the pole that is opposite to your front foot. Your pole plant should strike just after you place your front foot and begin transferring your weight. This counterbalancing will keep you upright and in control.

Sidestepping

Sometimes you need to move around an object that is in your way. You can do this by sidestepping. Pick up the leg on the side to which you are moving to a height just above the snow, move it sideways, then firmly plant it. Pick up the other snowshoe and bring it over next to the first one you moved. Voila!

Turning Around

Moving in reverse is exceedingly difficult in snowshoes. Snowshoes are balanced so that the toe points up and the tail swings down. It is very easy to dig the tail into the snow when trying to move it backward.

If you need to turn around, the easiest method is to **walk in a semicircle.** To do so, sidestep as above, but this time move your toe farther to one side than the heel, as if you are pivoting on the heel. You can do this sharply, or move forward as you turn. Be careful to pick up the snowshoe, turn it, and step down, as you do not want to dig

When you first put on your snowshoes, walk in a straight line to make sure your stride is comfortable and the snowshoes can move freely.

In deep snow a nice wide semicircle is an easy way to turn around.

the side of the snowshoe into the snow. To practice, start by walking in a circle, then see how small you can make the circle.

At some point in time you will find yourself in a position where walking in a semicircle is impossible. Whether in the forest surrounded by trees or on a steeper slope, the **kick turn** is the method of turning around that you will need to employ in this circumstance.

Kick turns are the best way to turn around when there is not enough room to walk in a semicircle.

The kick turn is easy to understand and only slightly more difficult to accomplish. First, plant your poles to your side. Then, pick up one foot and turn it 180 degrees around, so it is pointing in the exact opposite direction. Bring the pole on that side around and put your weight on that leg. To finish, pick up the other leg and rotate it so it is now facing in the same direction. Plant your poles, and you are now ready to move in the other direction.

Pacing

Pace yourself—what's the rush? Your day will be much more enjoyable if you move at a nice even clip. Walk as naturally as possible and stay balanced by taking smaller steps. By employing the **rest step** you can improve your efficiency. This method allows you to briefly transfer the weight from your leg muscles to your skeleton.

As you step forward and transfer all your weight to the front leg, lock your knee and take a brief pause. With the front leg locked, you can bring the back leg forward and do the same thing. It may be awkward at first, but once you get the hang of it, you'll be surprised at how much energy can be saved by using these brief rests.

In fresh snow **stamping** is another method to save energy. If you have spent much time around snow, you have certainly noticed that snow settles over time, becoming more compact and dense. You can re-create this process by pausing just for a moment as you step down on the top layer of snow. This will give the snow time to settle and compact, and your foot will not sink as deeply as if you had stepped down without pausing.

By waiting a moment to apply your weight after you initially step, you can "stamp" the snow. As the snow consolidates, you won't sink as far when you transfer your weight.

Breaking trail is fun and tiring. Lift your feet just enough to clear the snow, as extra movement wastes energy.

Breaking Trail

Breaking trail simply means snowshoeing in untouched snow. Breaking trail is fun, as you really are creating your own path, but it is much more exhausting. It might not slow you down in 3 inches of dense snow, but when breaking trail in a foot of fresh powder, be prepared for a workout!

When snowshoeing with other people, it is advantageous to rotate the person who is breaking trail on a fairly regular basis. People who are faster can break trail for longer periods of time as well, which will even out the pace and allow the slower folk to keep up in the back.

Finding the correct stride length and height is key to breaking trail efficiently. Make sure that each step falls just in front of the previous one, and only lift your leg high enough to step down evenly on the snow. There is no advantage to lifting your foot any higher.

Going Uphill

Snowshoes are amazing devices, but they are designed to go forward. Their helpfulness dramatically declines when traversing on uneven

The fall line can be visualized as the path a ball would travel if rolled down a slope. Often the fall line is the easiest way up.

terrain. Snowshoes pivot at one point, under the ball of the foot. When put on edge or set at an angle, the nearest flexible joint is your ankle. By using a snowshoe when your ankle is at a sideways angle, an incredible amount of traction is lost.

Ideally the fastest way to go up a hill is straight up the **fall line.** Think of this as the route a ball would take if allowed to roll from the top. The fall line is not only the shortest route, but is also the most likely place to find even footing.

A gentle rise will feel no different than going on flat terrain, but as soon as the pitch steepens, you will need to adjust your technique. Snow has a tendency to slide downhill. In order to prevent you from sliding down with it, you will need to apply more pressure under the ball of your foot in order to "set," or dig in, the crampon spikes. Think of climbing a ladder, pushing down on each rung. At the same time that your foot is pressing the snow in a downward direction, the snowshoe is freely rotating on the pivot bar/strap and will lie at the angle of the slope. This allows you to get a solid foothold with your foot while the snowshoe is still distributing your weight.

In uneven terrain, where moving straight up is impractical, you can use the **sidestep,** as discussed earlier. For any more than a few feet, however, this is impractical. So if you need to climb an incline that is just slightly too steep to approach it straight on, use the V-step.

The **V-step,** also known as the **herringbone step,** will give you more traction. By turning each foot out at a 45-degree angle, creating a wedge between your feet, more surface area will come in contact with the snowshoe. For short sections this can work well, but it is slow and tiring.

Generally the harder and denser the snow, the easier it is for your crampon spikes to dig in. This makes it easier to go straight up. If the pitch is just too steep and/or there is a significant amount of fresh snow, the next best option is to **switchback.** Instead of going straight up, you will zigzag up the slope. Although this increases the distance that you need to travel, it is more than compensated by the decrease in the angle of pitch.

Sidestepping is a straightforward method of climbing short hills but is not ideal in hard snow, super-deep snow, or any extended incline.

If you find your feet are sliding back when climbing a slope straight on, try V-stepping, which should give you more traction.

Although switchbacking increases your distance, it is often the most efficient way to climb steep hills.

Switchbacking actually works well in soft snow, where the snow can compress under your foot, providing a fairly even platform even though you are moving across the slope. The steeper the slope, the more you may need to angle each switchback. As you get a feel for it, try to find a good compromise between a reasonable angle and upward progress.

Going Downhill

You've worked hard to get up that hill, now it is time to have fun on your way down! Generally two factors affect your choice of descent method: snow type and angle. Deep snow, which is often a source of frustration while climbing, is a blast when going downhill. Hard, compact snow and icy conditions, which often create a quicker ascent, are the most difficult types of snow on which to descend.

When traveling downhill, make sure to use your poles. If your poles are extendable, it often helps to lengthen them for going downhill.

On a moderate decline you can step down as if you were walking down stairs, keeping your feet parallel to the horizon.

Poles can serve both to aid in balance and provide extra support. This removes some of the stress from your knees, which take a lot of force when moving downhill. Plant your poles firmly prior to making your step.

In fresh snow step straight down **as if you were going down a staircase.** Keep your feet and snowshoes parallel to the horizon and not at the angle of the slope. This will keep your balance more secure and put less weight on your knees. As you step down, the snow will compact under your snowshoe and will become like a stair upon which you can rest your weight. Depending on the angle of the slope, the size of your snowshoes, and the amount and consistency of the snow, your experience may vary. If you find the slope too steep, do not hesitate to switchback across it, increasing the distance traveled but reducing the force on your knees by slowing your descent.

If the snow is compacted or not very deep, or the terrain is icy, you may not have the luxury of keeping your feet parallel to the horizon. When this is the case, make sure that your crampons or other traction devices are firmly set prior to taking the next step. In these circumstances poles become even more important. Be vigilant in keeping your knees bent, and if you feel that you are losing control, stop and take a break.

Once you are comfortable going downhill at a controlled pace, there are two more techniques that are fun and fast ways to descend a slope. The first is a big step, or **leap step.** As you begin to descend quickly, make large steps down the hill, keeping your heel down and out in front. The additional force caused by the greater speed will force the snow to compact quickly and will hold up more weight. Eventually you will be comfortable running and leaping down the slope much faster than would be possible on dry ground. Keep in mind that snowshoes with fully free-pivoting bindings may have a tendency to dig the tail of the snowshoe into the snow, throwing off your balance. The more this is the case, the more important it is to put your weight on your heels.

If the hill is steep enough, one of the most fun ways to descend is by **glissading.** Glissading is like skiing on your snowshoes.

The joy of leaping down fresh powder snow makes the uphill work totally worthwhile.

Glissading involves keeping both feet on the ground and sliding down the hill. You can also sit down while descending, as this will give you more control.

Put your weight on your heels, keeping your snowshoes parallel. By keeping a wide stance, you will have more stability. As you weight your heels, allow yourself to slide down the hill. Make sure that there is a good run-out, as once you get going, the easiest and safest way to stop is by glissading down to terrain that is level.

Another method of glissading is to weight your heels as before, but this time bend your knees and put your butt on the snow. This allows you to use your hands as brakes and makes it easier to stop while being less likely to fall forward.

Getting Up from a Fall

Everybody falls and usually falls in snow are painless. The deeper the snow, the harder it may be to get up. When you do fall, before doing anything, take a deep breath and relax. Getting up can be exhausting, so allow yourself a chance to catch your breath.

Flat Ground

When you fall on flat ground, you will most likely just stop where you fall. If you fall face first, you may just be able to push yourself up into a kneeling position, as long as the snow is somewhat firm or not very deep. Generally, however, it is best to roll over on your back. Remember to take the pole straps off your wrists, but hold on to them. Lying on your back, lift your legs up out of the snow, then roll back over, making sure your knees and lower legs are in contact with the snow. Put your poles in an X out in front of you and then push against the poles, grabbing about one-third of the way down the shaft. After pushing off, you should have enough space below you to put one foot forward and push off that leg.

Steeper Terrain

When you fall on a hill, make sure you have stopped moving prior to trying to get up. If you fall with your legs downhill, turn over so that your chest is against the hill. Dig your toe crampons into the slope as deeply as possible to insure you do not slide down any farther. Once you've

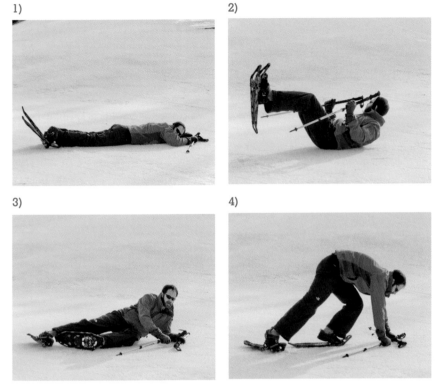

1)
2)
3)
4)

When you fall in deep snow, roll onto your back to free yourself of snow (2), then flip back over. To get up from any fall, starting on your stomach, place your poles in front of you in an X (3). Using this as leverage, you can move your foot forward and push to stand up (4).

got solid footing, you can work your upper body down the hill, keeping weight on the balls of your feet. Once in a kneeling position, put your poles in an X in front of you to push off. If it is steep, you may be able to immediately push against the slope to get yourself upright, using either your hands or your poles.

Falling face forward downhill can be an uncomfortable experience. Once you have stopped moving, make sure you are completely settled prior to trying to get up. Then shuffle your feet around below you, keeping your body in contact with the snow so that you do not slide. Once you have rotated by pivoting on your stomach, you can then get up using the method just described.

Things to Remember when Getting Up

When you get up from a prone position, do not dig in your poles with your hands on the grips to push yourself up. This puts a lot of force on your shoulders and could lead to injury. Also be sure to wipe all the snow from your clothing, face, and neck before you start moving. If snow went under your jacket, try to get as much of it out as possible prior to moving. Once you start moving, your body heat and friction will turn that snow into water, and once you are wet, you are much more likely to get cold.

Obstacles

Doubtless, if you snowshoe enough, you will come across obstacles. These often take the form of fallen trees, as well as rocks, streams, fences, drop-offs, etc. Use common sense when traveling past

You can step right over some downed trees, while you may need to step up onto others and then step down.

obstacles. Keep in mind that fallen trees may support snow, thereby obscuring holes or other dangers (more about this in chapter 5).

Trees are the most likely obstacles that you will encounter. The easiest approach, whenever feasible, is to go around it. If this is not possible, and the tree is too large to step over, you can step up onto the tree. Using the cleats on your bindings to grab into the trunk, move slowly, first bringing one foot up onto the trunk, then bringing the other on top, then stepping off. Do not place just the toe of the snowshoe onto the obstruction, as this is not a stable platform and could lead to a slip, possibly breaking the snowshoe . . . or you.

CHAPTER 4

More Advanced Snowshoeing Technique

As mentioned in the previous chapter, snowshoeing is a fairly straightforward endeavor. However, there are a few techniques beyond those discussed earlier that will allow you to travel in steeper and more varied terrain. As snowshoes can be used to both maintain traction and provide flotation and stability, they will allow you to travel on varied snow-covered terrain types.

Once you have become comfortable in snowshoes, tackle some steeper terrain and work on new techniques.

Steep Terrain

Once you are comfortable on easy and familiar terrain, it's time to venture out and explore. You will eventually find yourself on slopes that may be too steep to easily walk up using straight stepping or the V-step, and even switchbacking may be difficult due to the pitch and type of snow. Below are a few tips that will help you ascend and descend steep slopes.

Toe Kicking

When the terrain steepens it becomes increasingly important to make sure that the cleats/crampons under the ball of your foot are set into something solid. Toe kicking is exactly what it sounds like. Instead of just stepping and placing your feet, swing your foot into the side of the hill with some force. It may take more than one try before you get solid footing, so keep on swinging your toe into the hill until you are sure it is firmly planted.

On steep slopes with little snow, or on snow that is hard and there is ice, it will be obvious when you have a good connection with the ground. It is much more difficult, and much less safe, to toe kick when the snow is deep and unconsolidated.

There are two flavors of toe kicking. Most of the time you will be able to swing your foot into the slope with enough force to gain a solid foothold. However, when the terrain gets very steep, you will want to angle your

On steep, slick terrain kick your snowshoe forward until you can feel your crampons bite into the snow.

toe down enough so that not only your foot but the entire toe of the snowshoe digs in. The greater the angle of rotation allowed by your binding, the harder it will be to do this, but doing so gives you more surface area in contact with the stable underlayer of the snow. This provides more traction.

Side Kicking for Straight Climbing and Traversing

As mentioned earlier, if a slope is too steep to comfortably ascend, you can switchback, or traverse the slope at an angle. This creates a lower-angle ascent so that the elevation is gained over a longer distance. On steep slopes, however, this can be awkward, and it may be very difficult to get the snowshoe to sit flat on the snow. As soon as your ankle turns at an angle, you have much less stability and a greater chance of losing traction. It is therefore important for each step to be as level to the horizon as possible.

When traversing a slope that is too steep to easily walk or even sidestep, side kicking is the next option. You want to make sure your footing is solid before lifting a snowshoe and making another step. To make sure you have solid footing, step forward and swing your leg across your body into the slope. Force the side of the snowshoe hard into the side of the slope. This should dig in the snowshoe, creating enough of a platform to both support your weight and allow at least some of your crampon spikes to dig in. The steeper the terrain or harder

Walk across and up a slope if it is too steep to comfortably climb straight up.

the snow, the more force you will need to apply in order to get a solid footing.

To gain elevation, you may need to put your back foot uphill and forward of the front foot. This may feel uncomfortable at first, especially when bringing your downhill leg around.

You can also use this technique to climb straight up short steep sections. Instead of bringing the downhill leg and foot forward and above the uphill leg, just bring it up next to the uphill leg. Once you have a solid footing, you can move the uphill leg farther out and uphill before bringing the downhill leg up again.

For both techniques, make sure to switch the direction that you are facing at regular intervals, as it is important to not fatigue one leg unduly.

Going Down Steep Terrain

Chapter 3 discusses the most common techniques for going downhill.

If the terrain becomes very steep, however, you may need to apply the side-kicking traverse technique to move across and down the hill. Do the same thing as mentioned above for side kicking, forcing the side of the snowshoe into the side of the hill, swinging your foot into the slope one or more times until you have a solid foothold. The only difference is that this time your back leg will swing around and down ahead of your front foot. You can also do the same thing with smaller steps, leading with the same foot each time.

If the terrain is too steep to comfortably descend in control,

If the descent gets steep, take your time, making sure each step is secure.

find another way down that may be longer but less steep. Yes, rolling down a hill may be the fastest way, but unless you are a good bowler, it is better to stay on your feet and find a safe alternative route.

Running and Racing

Running with snowshoes is a tiring endeavor, but it is a blast. It is a fun way to enjoy the outdoors and get in shape at the same time. And for those with a competitive side, snowshoe racing can be found at venues across this country and beyond.

Running in snowshoes can be an awkward affair in fresh snow, but on packed terrain with small snowshoes, it can be a great workout.

What's better than snowshoe racing? Snowshoe racing with dogs!

In general, snowshoes used for running are small and lightweight and can even be side-specific. As most snowshoe race courses, and snowshoe running trails for that matter, are packed down, a large snowshoe for flotation is unnecessary. Instead, the snowshoes serve to add traction and provide a solid surface from which to rebound for the next stride. Ideally the degree of rotation allowed by the binding is fairly limited. A binding that allows the snowshoe to pivot too much prevents the snowshoe and foot from hitting the ground at the same time, which can cause the tail to dig into snow, tripping up the runner.

In order to keep the overall weight down, you will most likely be served best by wearing sneakers. I think the motto "A pound on the foot is five on the back" is appropriate here. This means that by adding an additional pound of weight on your feet, you will expend the same amount of energy as you would by adding five pounds to your backpack weight. Though this will vary from person to person, it is generally best to use the lightest shoes that will keep your feet warm and dry. (Interestingly, slightly colder conditions will keep your feet drier, and therefore warmer, than near-freezing temps where water becomes a problem.)

Keep in mind that when running with snowshoes, you will burn more calories than a similar run on dry ground. Also, make sure to stretch after a short warm-up. Cold makes muscles tight and stiff, and without proper stretching you may be more likely to pull a muscle. Stretch when you are finished as well.

Look online to see if there are any official races in your area. You can also check out the resources at the back of this book to find possible races. The United States Snowshoe Association website (www .snowshoeracing.com) contains many listings of races across the country.

CHAPTER 5

Be Aware and Stay Safe

In order to have an enjoyable outing on snowshoes, it is important to understand the safety considerations associated with any outdoor endeavor as well as those associated with snowshoeing in particular. Whereas a mishap in the summer is usually not serious, there are many more risks associated with traveling in the winter. Shorter days, colder temperatures, snow issues, and remoteness are just a few of the factors that make a winter adventure a greater undertaking than a similar trip in warmer weather. Always tell someone you trust where you are going and when you expect to return. If something serious happens while you are out, people need to know where to find you.

Snowshoe outings can range from short jaunts on packed trails to remote backcountry adventures spanning many days. Obviously each endeavor has particular risks associated with it, and this book is not meant to cover all the things to think about in a remote adventure. There is no need to be scared, however. By being aware and prepared, and by understanding techniques to stay safe, you will be much more likely to have an enjoyable trip, even if there are no specific safety concerns.

Additionally, one of the best ways to get information on terrain, snow concerns, and other obstacles is by talking with somebody who has recent experience traveling over the same terrain. Most winter resorts have helpful staff, and many

Be very wary when approaching streams banked by snow, as the edge may not support your weight. Take your time to find the safest way to cross.

guidebooks point out the possible areas of concern. You may also run across people while you are out. Don't be afraid to ask them what may lie ahead and whether or not there is anything to be aware of. Finally, the Internet now contains many regularly updated condition reports and forums full of people sharing their experiences. A little research can go a long way in making your trip a safe and enjoyable one.

Snow Types and Terminology

Natives of arctic regions, such as the Sami people in Northern Europe, have hundreds of words for snow. That should give you a clue as to the wide range of snow types that exist and the importance this has in the ease of snow travel. Below you will find a list of some common snow-related terms with explanations of what they mean and, where appropriate, how they can relate to your snowshoeing expectations.

- **Base depth/snowpack** refers to the distance from the top of the snow to the bare ground, usually measured in centimeters or inches. Deeper snow makes snowshoeing more difficult and slower.

- **Surface type** refers to the consistency of snow found on the top layer, or surface, of the snow.

- **Density** refers to the amount of water contained in a given amount of snow. The denser the snow, the more weight it can support and the less it will compact when stepped on.

- **Powder** usually refers to light, fluffy snow that is not very dense but can also refer to fresh snow of any type.

- **Crust** is a hard consolidated layer that forms when a layer of snow melts and then freezes, or rain hits snow and freezes. This can be on the top of the snow, but freezing events from earlier points in the season can create layers of crust which fall below the surface. Crust can be just millimeters deep or be as thick as many inches.

- **Layers** are formed when different temperatures and conditions create different snow types. As these snow types fall on top of each other

The colder the temperature, the more likely the snow will be light and fluffy. Depending upon how deep the snowpack is, dry unconsolidated snow can make for an exhausting snowshoe.

In locations such as the high Sierra in California, snow lasts through much of the summer. In the mornings the snow is hard, and the crampons underfoot come in handy, but by late afternoon the snow is so soft that it feels like moving through sand.

You never know what you'll find when you snowshoe in the mountains. Here, rime ice and wind-sculpted snow called "sastrugi" coat everything.

and temperatures fluctuate, the snow builds into layers, with some denser than others. Understanding layers, especially on sloped terrain, is key to analyzing avalanche concerns.

- **Granular** refers to snow that has gone through varying temperature cycles. Instead of individual flakes, granular snow manifests as small balls of ice. You will likely come across granular snow when snowshoeing in the spring or summer.

- **Slush** refers to any snow that is consolidated and near or above freezing, so that it becomes very heavy and wet. It is slush that is most likely to soak your feet.

- **Slope angle** refers to the steepness of a slope. The higher the angle, the steeper the slope. Lower-angle slopes hold snow better, and certain angles are more likely to have avalanche concerns.

- **Sun cups** occur in the spring and summer when temperatures rise above freezing. As the snow melts, it pools. These pools are darker than the surrounding snow and therefore collect

Wind can scour a surface of all its snow, leaving just a frozen crust.

more heat during the day. As these little pools heat up, they get more water and the pools grow in size. The net effect of this is a pockmarked surface with circular depressions divided by sharp ridges. Sun cups can make traveling very difficult.

Other considerations when looking at conditions include whether the trail is already packed down, either by foot traffic or a groomer, or whether the snow is unbroken and fresh. Ice can also take many forms, from small granular balls to hard compacted snow to clear ice, similar to black ice on the roads.

As you spend more time snowshoeing, you will become acquainted with the implications of snow types to safety and energy expenditure.

Sun cups form when water melts, creating little dark pools that absorb more heat than the surrounding snow.

Snow Dangers

Dangers related to snow come in all varieties, but there are two main issues of concern. One involves the hidden dangers below the surface of the snow. The other involves avalanches, a serious concern for anybody traveling in mountainous snow-covered terrain. A third danger, the Abominable Snowman, is not a real concern in most locales.

Hidden Dangers

One of the most alluring aspects of snow is the fact that it makes the terrain look even and smooth. Even a small snow cover can turn a rough, jumbled brown setting into a place of magical beauty. However, any time snow covers the ground, it is obscuring possible dangers. The deeper the snowpack, the more hidden hazards.

It is extremely important to be aware when crossing over **water** or **frozen water.** Snow may cover water that is only lightly frozen or even open and running. Understand where and when you will be crossing over water. Be sure any frozen body of water has thick enough ice to

Moving water may not be obvious when traveling over frozen terrain, so be extra careful when snowshoeing near rivers and lakes.

Test the stability of any snow bridge before using it to cross a river, as the bridge may be undermined by the moving water.

support crossing it. Many small streams can be crossed with a long stride or jump.

Snow bridges are exactly what they sound like. Snow can be carved away by running water underneath, and snow may naturally cover up an opening below. Try avoiding crossing on obvious snow bridges. When you must, be sure to test the snow with a pole, then a single foot prior to putting your entire weight on it. Look for possible exit areas in case the bridge does collapse. If temperatures have been above freezing for any extended period of time, be even more suspect of the bridges.

Hidden obstacles, such as **downed trees and rocks,** may lurk below the surface of the snow. Often fallen trees can support snow, leaving a hole below the branches and the bottom of the snow. Look for any irregularities on the surface of the snow to note where these may lie. Rocks, being darker than the snow, heat up much faster than the snow on warm, sunny days. The hot rock in turn melts the snow that is closest to it. Often the snow near rocks becomes **undermined,** leaving the surface fairly untouched but creating a hole underneath. When snowshoeing near exposed rocks, especially on warm days, stay far from the edges of the rocks.

In addition to downed trees being a hidden obstacle, trees can also present two other dangers. First, **tree wells** are formed when the canopy of a tree prevents snow from accumulating at the base. Tree wells are noted by a deep ring of much shallower snow around the trunk, with walls of snow just beyond the protection of the canopy. Tree wells can be very deep and are often rather difficult to extricate oneself from. If tree wells are present, stay at least a few feet beyond

As branches shield the base of the trees from snow, a depression, or "well," develops, which rings the trunk. Tree wells can be very deep, so in a deep snowpack, steer clear of the trunks.

the wall. (Small tree wells, on the other hand, can provide dry ground or shelter from the wind and snow and can be great spots for breaks.)

The second obstacle that can be created by living trees is **hidden branches.** Evergreen trees, such as fir trees, keep their needles or leaves throughout the year, and snow piling up on tree limbs may appear as solid ground. In places where there is a deep snowpack, much of the tree may be hidden, creating the false impression that the tree is much shorter than it really is. Since the base of the tree is wider than the tip, be careful as you approach a tree. Snow surrounding the trunk may not be able to support your weight. If you are unsure, be safe and stay a good distance from the trunk of the tree.

Avalanches

One of the most dangerous facets of hiking in snow-covered mountains is avalanches. Entire books have been written about this subject, and classes are taught around the world on proper ways to evaluate avalanche hazard and travel in terrain that is susceptible to avalanches. The best method for surviving an avalanche is to not get in one in the first place.

Here at Big Sky in Montana, ski patrollers regularly dig snow pits and use specialty tools to determine whether a slope is safe and unlikely to slide in an avalanche.

There are many different types of avalanches, but the basic definition of an avalanche involves a large amount of snow sliding down the mountain. The three main types of avalanches are slab avalanches; sluff, or loose snow, avalanches; and wet avalanches. These are described below, but you can find much more in-depth information on avalanches online and in books.

Slab avalanches are the most deadly type of avalanche. They occur when a harder or more cohesive snow sets up on top of a softer or weaker snow or a layer of frozen snow/ice. A lower layer of snow cannot support the layer on top, and when this support breaks, a large amount of snow can suddenly start dropping down the mountain. Slab avalanches can occur naturally, but many of the deadliest avalanches are triggered by humans. A small amount of weight or a line cut by a ski or snowshoe track can be the impetus for collapsing the support. Slab avalanches can often be noted by a distinct fracture line.

Sluff, or loose snow, avalanches occur when gravity pulls unconsolidated snow down a mountain. This is usually caused by

Slides such as this send anywhere from hundreds to thousands of tons of snow down the mountain, destroying anything in their path.

the natural incline of the slope and will often accompany a skier or snowshoer while traveling downhill. Although not usually deadly, large sluff avalanches can definitely cause trouble.

Wet avalanches usually occur in spring and summer conditions. When warm temperatures melt the snow and saturate it with water, the bonds holding the snow together deteriorate. When enough water has melted and the terrain is steep enough, the top surface of dense wet snow can come sliding down the mountain.

Tips to Stay Safe from Avalanches

- **Stay in the trees.** Although not a sure thing, the presence of trees on a slope may signify that no avalanches large enough to tear down the trees have occurred there. Additionally, trees can help maintain the stability of a snowpack. Snowshoeing in the trees is one of the best ways to stay safe in mountainous snow-covered terrain.

Avalanches can be deadly, so be informed about the avalanche danger before wandering out into snow-covered mountainous terrain.

- **Analyze slope angle.** Avalanches usually occur on slopes that are steep enough to pull the snow downhill. Although they can occur on any slopes, slopes between the angles of 30 and 60 degrees are the most dangerous. Flat or slightly sloped terrain is the least likely place to avalanche.

- **Be most concerned about untouched snow.** If you are the first person to travel on a slope, be very careful. Once a number of people have been through an area without incident, it is much less likely an avalanche will occur. Don't be a guinea pig!

- **Monitor reports.** There are many online resources available for finding out avalanche danger. Check to see if there are any reports on the area you will be traveling. Places that are hotbeds for backcountry skiing often have these reports, which are usually rated on a scale from "safe" to "extremely dangerous."

- **Talk with knowledgeable locals.** The best sources of information about avalanche danger are often locals who know the area well. Don't be afraid to ask around. Often outdoor sporting good stores are staffed with knowledgeable people who will know the answers to your questions.

Transceivers, or beacons, such as the one shown here, are vital pieces of gear in avalanche terrain. When all parties have these, it allows rescuers to find buried victims. Probes and shovels are also important in finding and recovering victims.

When traveling in avalanche terrain, nothing is more important than proper training and equipment. **Avalanche beacons** are electronic devices worn on the chest that transmit and receive signals that allow people to find buried victims (assuming all parties have beacons). **Probes** are collapsible metal poles used to narrow down the location of the buried victim. **Collapsible shovels** allow a rescuer to quickly dig for the victim. New equipment such as backpacks with airbags that deploy to float a victim to the surface and breathing apparatuses that send air around behind a victim, preventing suffocation by carbon dioxide, are also gaining popularity with people who travel in steep avalanche-prone terrain.

When an avalanche stops, the snow can be as hard and thick as concrete. Many victims have died just inches below the surface. If you get caught in an avalanche, try to move, or "swim," your way sideways to get out of the path. Continue to move your arms, and do your best to stay near the surface. *Never travel alone in avalanche-prone terrain.*

Temperature and Weather

Knowledge is the best tool for staying safe. Before heading out on any winter adventure, check the weather. Think about how the temperature will affect your comfort and remember that if

In the summer bad weather can be an inconvenience. In the winter it can be much more serious. Be aware of your environment, and if the weather looks questionable, make sure you are in a safe, sheltered location . . . preferably with a hot chocolate in hand.

snowshoeing in the mountains, the temperature may be significantly colder than that reported on the news or in the paper. It is often much windier in the mountains and on wide open spaces.

Windchill is the effect that wind has on the way temperature feels. If it is going to be windy, be sure to wear windproof clothing. Prepare for the windchill temperature, not the actual temperature. A nice 25-degree day can be quite miserable if accompanied by 25-mph winds. The National Oceanic and Atmospheric Administration has a good windchill chart (www.nws.noaa.gov/om/windchill). See, for example, that 25 degrees will feel like 9 degrees with a 25-mph wind.

Tips to Prepare for Snowshoeing in Cold Weather

Hypothermia and frostbite are the two main concerns to be aware of when traveling in cold weather. **Hypothermia** is a condition where your body is losing more heat than it is producing. Normal body temperature is around 98.6 degrees; hypothermia occurs when your body temperature drops below 95 degrees. Severe hypothermia, at body temperatures below 90 degrees, can lead to the shutting down of vital organs.

Frostbite occurs when your body gets very cold, naturally pulling the circulation away from the extremities to keep your core warm. In turn, the toes, fingers, ears, and nose are usually the first parts of the body to feel the effects of frostbite. When skin and the body tissue underneath the skin freezes, it makes the affected area numb, hard, and pale. Minor frostbite can be treated by slowly warming the affected area, but severe frostbite can lead to the death of tissue and even amputation of the affected area.

Below are a number of tips to help prevent cold-related maladies.

- **Layering:** By layering with numerous lighter weight garments, as opposed to a few thick garments, you will be able to adjust to varying conditions as appropriate.

- **Gloves, hats, and face masks:** When cold, your extremities are the first places where you will begin to feel the effects. Additionally, much heat can be lost through the head, and the simple act of donning a hat can aid tremendously in keeping your whole body warm. Face masks and balaclavas will keep your ears and cheeks warm.

- **Waterproofing footwear and external garments:** Like fingers, toes are extremities, and when you get cold, your toes are often the first things to feel it. When your feet get wet, they are much more likely to get cold and freeze. Most winter hiking boots are waterproof, but it never hurts to apply waterproofing spray or liquid to the outside of the boots to maintain them. This can be bought at any outdoor goods store. Similarly, external garments that are meant to be waterproof can lose this ability over time. Wash-in waterproofing for these fabrics can also be purchased at outdoor stores.

- **Constant vigilance:** Other than having proper clothing, being vigilant about your body temperature is one of the most important factors in staying warm and comfortable. If you get cold, deal with it immediately because postponing your response will make it much more likely that you will suffer cold-related symptoms later on.

- **Don't sweat:** If you work hard, or wear too much clothing, you will sweat. Once you stop, the evaporating moisture will rapidly remove heat from your body, and wet clothing does not insulate nearly as well. If you begin to sweat, slow down or remove some clothing so you stay dry.

- **Windmilling:** To regain circulation in your fingers, spin your arms around as if you were throwing a fast softball pitch, again and again. The centripetal force sends blood to the extremities and will warm your fingers quickly.

- **Monitor your snowshoeing partner(s):** When extremities get cold, they will first turn red, and once frostbite starts to occur, the affected area will begin to turn a pale white. Constantly check each other to make sure nobody is getting frostbitten. Also be sure to ask one another how you are feeling, as people's temperature regulation and comfort threshold vary dramatically. Don't be afraid to speak up, as a five-minute stop to deal with cold issues will prevent much more costly and time-consuming issues in the future.

- **Be aware of changing conditions:** When you are snowshoeing and are caught up in the moment, it is easy not to notice changing temperatures and weather conditions. Always check the weather before you leave and constantly monitor conditions. If conditions are deteriorating, turn around and head back or get to shelter. Many people now carry small thermometers to monitor the temperature.

- **Cloudy or clear, day or night:** Although sunny days often provide warmer temperatures, the cloudless sky will not retain the earth's reflected heat. Cloudy days usually have much more stable temperatures, whereas clear nights are usually much colder. If you plan on being out at night, bring much warmer clothing.

- **Drink and eat plenty:** Food is fuel, and as this fuel is burned, it creates heat. Hydration can help prevent many maladies. Drink plenty of water before you leave and while on the trail. By staying hydrated your body has the means to regulate temperature better. Remember, by the time you are thirsty, you are already partly dehydrated, so drink even if you aren't thirsty. (Eating snow will *not* hydrate you, as you use

Conditions can change rapidly in the winter.

Clouds trap re-radiated heat from the earth, keeping nighttime temperatures from dramatically dropping. Clear, starry nights are usually the coldest nights in winter.

more energy and water to melt the snow in your body than you get from consuming it.)

- **Listen to great music:** Just seeing if you are paying attention!

Weather-related Concerns

Because one often snowshoes in mountainous environments or during the winter (or both), there are a number of weather concerns that must considered before venturing out on a journey. Temperatures are often cold and the length of daylight is usually much shorter in the winter.

Mountain environments are known for rapidly changing weather. Monitor the forecast before heading out, but always be prepared to **expect the unexpected.** Make sure to pack everything you might need if the weather deteriorates. Snow, rain, sleet, hail, and freezing rain are all possible, and even a sunny day can rapidly turn to stormy weather in the mountains.

In the winter expect the unexpected and prepare for all types of weather. Fog forms in winter over open water.

When it is snowing hard, fresh snow can pile up rapidly. Fresh snow is usually lighter and less consolidated. More snow requires more work, so make sure to constantly analyze the situation and realize that if it keeps snowing, you may not get to your destination in a timely manner. Heavy snow or fog can also create a whiteout. A whiteout means a loss of visibility due to moisture in the air or heavily falling snow. When a whiteout occurs, it is very difficult to navigate, and traveling in whiteout conditions should be avoided whenever possible.

CHAPTER 6

Fun for Everyone!

One of the factors that make snowshoeing so much fun is that anyone can do it. If you can walk, you can snowshoe. Snowshoes are relatively inexpensive compared to other winter sports equipment and can often be rented for a minimal expense if you look around hard enough. Snowshoeing is a great way to share the outdoors with family and friends, young and old, accompanied by furry companions, and in large groups or out on your own.

Snowshoeing with Children

Snowshoeing is a great way to get children to enjoy the outdoors. It's more exciting than a plain old walk. It is

People of all shapes and sizes can enjoy snowshoeing.

important to keep in mind, though, that snowshoeing is tiring, and a 1-foot snowpack can be thigh deep for a small child.

The best way to enjoy your time snowshoeing with children is to make sure that they are comfortable, have energy, and, most important, are having fun. Play in the snow, create adventure games, and use the adventure as a teaching experience to explore nature.

Manufacturers now make snowshoes in children's sizes.

Many snowshoe manufacturers make children's snowshoes, and often discount stores will have cheap plastic snowshoes that will serve the purpose just fine. Children grow so quickly, it makes little sense to buy expensive small snowshoes, only for them to be too small the following year. When learning, the priority is that the snowshoes stay on their feet, allowing the kids to understand what it feels like.

Can't get your kids to go on hikes? Put snowshoes on them, because everything's more fun in the snow!

Below is a list of things to consider when planning a snowshoe outing involving children.

- **Keep the mileage down.** Nobody wants to hike with a happy, energetic child only to get to a point far away from the beginning/end and have the child become upset due to exhaustion. Start with small loops near the car or house, and gradually work toward longer excursions once you know the stamina of the child.

- **Use the experience to learn about the outdoors.** Winter is a great time to learn about animal tracks. Bring along a guidebook and learn with the child. Look for feathers and try to figure out what type of bird may be flying over the snow. Play geography lessons and teach the child how to read a map. Be actively engaging throughout the outing. (Also tell funny jokes.)

- **Let them carry some of their own gear.** Whether using a small backpack or a fanny pack, allowing children to carry some of their own gear, even just water and snacks, will both give them a sense of accomplishment and train them to understand that heading out into nature requires you to be prepared.

Make sure the snowshoes are snug, as children can work their way out of anything.

Kids love making snow angels.

- **Stop for snacks.** Most adults can go for a number of hours without eating, or even feeling the need to eat. Children should eat much more often to make sure they have the reserves needed to make it the whole way. Also make sure they get plenty to drink. (Providing hot chocolate in a thermos is a great way to get kids to drink.)

- **Create small goals.** "Okay, let's see who can get to that rock" or "At the next viewpoint, let's have some hot chocolate." Incentivize the trip, and turn it into a number of small trips. Children may be overwhelmed when they hear a snowshoe loop is 1 mile, but it will seem much less intimidating if they are only thinking about getting to that next rock or tree.

- **Bring a sled.** By associating snowshoeing with a fun activity such as sledding, children will be more likely to want to go out on another adventure. A sled with some rope also gives the adult companion(s) the ability to put a tired child in the sled and pull him or her home.

Let children fall and play in the snow, but make sure that they aren't getting cold or wet and that they haven't left any gear behind.

- **Play games.** Make snow angels, have races, build snowmen, and have snowball tosses. This will make the trip more fun for everyone.

- **Make sure they are comfortable and warm.** Keep a vigilant eye on the child, looking for signs of cold such as shivering, white spots on the skin, and blue lips. A child may not be able to accurately convey his or her comfort level, so it is imperative that the adult constantly asks how the child is feeling and is responsive to both stated and unstated signs.

- **Before leaving, check all gear.** Once you have the child outfitted, double-check to make sure that the snowshoes won't come off, the clothing is comfortable, and everything else works as it should.

Learn to identify animals by their tracks. A deer print is clearly identifiable in the new snow.

Snowshoeing with Dogs

You may not always have a person to accompany you on your snowshoe, but dogs are always willing to go on an adventure. It is important for an owner to understand the fitness and comfort level of his or her dog. Some dogs are meant for long distances and some are not. Long-haired dogs usually fare much better in cold temperatures than do short-haired varieties.

When snowshoeing with dogs, it is important that they are responsive to the owner's commands. Dogs do not necessarily understand when they are in a dangerous situation. This is especially true when nearing or crossing frozen or moving water.

There are a number of things one can do to ensure that a snowshoe adventure is fun and safe for both the dogs and the people.

- **Keep an eye on their feet.** By far the biggest issue to be concerned about while out snowshoeing with a dog is the condition of its feet. Cold snow and ice can be very abrasive to the pads on the bottom of the dog's feet. Additionally, wet snow can clump up in between the pads and stick to the fur between

Dogs are great companions on a snowshoe, and sometimes they'll even break trail for you.

the dog's toes. Dogs are usually able to deal with clumping themselves by picking it out with their teeth. Check to make sure this is the case, and give your dog a chance to do this by stopping occasionally.

- **Use salve or booties.** If you know or think your dog is going to have problems, you can purchase specific snow booties for him or her at many pet shops and outdoor goods stores. You may also be able to find salve, such as Musher's Secret, that safeguards the dog's pads by coating them with a protective layer. Salve can also aid in the recovery of the dog's feet.

Putting on salve, such as Musher's Secret, helps prevent the pads on your dog's feet from becoming irritated by ice and snow.

- **Bring some treats or extra food.** Just like humans, dogs need food for energy. Keep in mind that your dog may be working

Dogs can usually clean out their own paws of clumped ice and snow, but if they can't, it can be painful, so be sure to keep an eye on your dog's feet.

much harder than you, since you have snowshoes and the dog sinks in the snow. If you are going out for a while, especially if in deep snow or very cold temperatures, give the dog some treats throughout the hike. Food provides more energy for walking and heating, and can be a good incentive for behaving well.

- **Use doggie jackets for short-haired dogs.** If your dog has short hair or is prone to getting cold, you can find nice warm coats that wrap around the body at many pet stores.

- **During hunting season, use bright orange.** Hunting season, which overlaps with the snow season in many locales, means that you will be snowshoeing while hunters are out looking for animals. Make sure a hunter doesn't mistake your dog for a deer or other animal by putting a bright orange vest on him. If it is a real concern, put a small bell on the dog collar.

- **Dogs can eat snow to hydrate . . . usually.** In most circumstances dogs, unlike humans, can eat snow for hydration. When temperatures are really cold, however, dogs will need liquid water, as melting the snow by body heat cools the core temperature and wastes energy.

Jackets and booties made specifically for dogs can help keep them warm and prevent uncomfortable irritations on their feet. Short-haired dogs are more likely to need the extra insulation.

- **Check their fur for ice balls.** As with the feet, fur that is in contact with wet snow may clump up with ice balls that, once formed, continue to grow. These pull at the dog's fur and can be very uncomfortable. When possible, help remove these clumps, which often form on the hindquarters and under the belly.

- **Use a dog pack.** Yes, there are packs for dogs too. In addition to relieving you from having to carry gear for the dog, the extra weight may slow him down enough to prevent him from getting too far ahead. These packs also usually have handles that can help you lift a dog when needed.

Snowshoeing for People with Disabilities

Of the multitude of winter activities, snowshoeing is one of the most accessible. Everyone can enjoy the wonders of winter through snowshoeing, which provides exercise and a sense of accomplishment.

When accompanying people with significant disabilities, make sure they are comfortable, safe, and enjoying the outing. Allow them to discover the best way to travel through snow on their own, while providing positive encouragement and feedback throughout. They may express their discomforts or problems with their equipment in a different manner, so it is important that you are aware of an individual's abilities and means of communicating prior to embarking on an outdoor adventure.

Snowshoeing is for everyone, and nothing is better than sharing a wonderful winter experience.

Traveling in a Group

Snowshoeing with friends and family can be a greatly rewarding experience. Very few winter activities are as accessible as snowshoeing, and sharing the experience can make it that much more enjoyable. The most important aspect to enjoying a snowshoe outing with a group is to have similar expectations, keeping in mind

Snowshoeing is one of the easiest outdoor activities to share in a group. Keep the needs and expectations of all in mind, and if young children are included, stay near your home base.

various ages, fitness levels, and desires. All parties should have a good experience.

- **Share expectations and goals.** Nothing is more important for having a successful group outing than to be open and honest about everyone's goals and expectations. Plan a route that even the oldest or least fit member will enjoy.

- **In fresh snow, put the strongest members first.** It takes much more energy to break trail in fresh snow. By putting the strongest member(s) out front, it should help even out the speed.

- **On packed trails, have the slower members lead.** Putting the slowest member of the group first ensures that nobody is moving too fast.

- **Stronger members should carry more load.** To even out the pace, have the fastest members of the group carry more of the group gear, such as first-aid supplies and food.

The author catches a sunrise on a solo snowshoe up Mount Moosilauke.

Traveling Alone

Snowshoeing by yourself can be one of the most rewarding outdoor experiences. The quiet of traveling solo allows you to really appreciate your surroundings. It also provides the opportunity to both move at a pace of your own choosing and stop and start at your own leisure. However, traveling alone can be a riskier proposition, and there are a number of steps you should take to make your trip a safe and enjoyable one.

- **Share your route with someone you trust.** If anything happens to you while you are out, it is vital that people know where you are going. Share your route with someone you trust who will be prepared to take action if something goes wrong. It is even better to share your route with multiple people. Also share your estimated travel time, allowing for minor unexpected delays. Write this down on a piece of paper.

- **Bring a phone.** You might not always have cell coverage, but if you do, a phone can be a lifesaver when traveling alone. Many new phones also contain a GPS, allowing you to inform rescuers exactly where you are located.

- **Travel only in safe terrain.** The consequences of something going awry while you are alone are much more severe than in a group. Do not travel in avalanche terrain or over frozen bodies of water unless you are 100 percent certain that the area is safe.

- **Carry important safety and navigation gear.** Make sure you have dry clothing, food, water, a map, a lighter or matches, and a headlamp, as well as other important first-aid gear.

- **Travel in daylight.** It is much more difficult to navigate in the dark, so when traveling alone, make sure to arrive at your destination before darkness falls.

Etiquette, Manners, Good Sense

When snowshoeing in locations where you will run across other people, it is important to observe a number of rules of thumb. Through following simple rules of etiquette, you will make the experience safe and enjoyable for everyone.

- **Make sure you have permission.** This is common sense. Unless the land is public land, it is necessary to make sure that you have the right to be snowshoeing on that property. Many resorts allow you to snowshoe in specific areas. By disobeying these rules, you may jeopardize not only your trip, but also the rights of snowshoers who might follow you.

- **Don't ruin cross-country ski trails.** Cross-country skiers rely on tracks from groomers

Some trails are multiuse. Allow people on skis to pass if they are moving more quickly, and if there is a ski track, keep your snowshoe prints off to the side.

Snowmobile tracks can make snowshoeing a breeze. Just make sure to get out of their way if you hear them coming.

or prior skiers to make their trip smooth and efficient. There is nothing a skier dislikes more than to come across a nice trail that has been destroyed by a snowshoer.

- **Share the trail.** Other users may be on the trail. If people come up from behind who are clearly faster than you or your group, step aside and let them pass.

- **Don't leave any trash, even food scraps.** Leave the land as you found it. Never leave trash behind, even if it is biodegradable. Food scraps do not break down in the winter and may invite unwanted critters.

- **Allow plenty of room for snowmobiles to pass.** If you are traveling on a snowmobile trail, remember that you are on their route. If you hear or see a snowmobile coming, step off to the side of the trail to let it pass.

Choosing Where to Go

If there is snow, you can snowshoe! Unlike many other winter activities, snowshoeing can be done just about anywhere. As long as there is enough snow to make snowshoeing worthwhile, put them on and get going. There are better and worse places to snowshoe, though, so here are some suggestions.

Hiking trails covered in snow become snowshoe trails in winter. As long as the trails do not involve crazy rock scrambling, you can use pretty much any hiking guidebook as a starting point for your snowshoe adventure. Keep in mind that many trails may get icy in winter, so you may need a snowshoe that has good crampon spikes. Some trails may be closed in winter, so make sure you have permission to use it. During transition seasons you may only need snowshoes for those parts of the trail that are covered in snow. Stay off the trails if they are muddy, as using muddy trails causes enormous erosion.

Make sure to give yourself enough time to get back to your car. In most places in the United States, winter means much shorter days, so your available light is much diminished. Additionally, always assume you will be moving much slower on snowshoes than you would on dry ground, so be sure to add additional time to account for this.

Now that you can walk on snow, there are so many more adventures ahead.

Want a big winter adventure? Take snowshoeing to the next level, and camp out with the snow.

In addition to traditional hiking resources, there are now many books on good snowshoe trails. By using established trails, there is a likelihood that other people will or have used the trail, thus creating a packed surface that will be much faster. There will also be less likelihood of encountering unexpected obstacles when traveling on a trail.

When there is enough snow, you can also create your own path. Unlike hiking, going off-trail when there is enough snow is not detrimental to the life there. If you do decide to head off into the woods on an off-trail adventure, it is imperative that you know where you are and where you are going, and that you give yourself ample time to get back safely.

Frozen lakes and ponds are also great places to snowshoe. As long as you are certain the water is completely frozen and safe for travel, these flat open spaces are the perfect spots for using large traditional snowshoes, as flotation is more important than maneuverability.

Resorts and outdoor centers are also good places to go snowshoeing. They often have trails dedicated to snowshoeing and these are usually loops, avoiding a return on the same trail. These trails are usually packed down as well, which will allow you to cover more distance and not waste energy traveling in fresh snow.

See you on the snow!

Resources

Traditional hiking and snowshoeing guidebooks are great references for choosing an adventure. If you are in a place that you don't know well, go to the local outdoor goods store or even general store to see if you can get information from local residents.

There are many sites available online to aid snowshoers, and by doing a search, you will quickly find the information you need. A few organizations focus on all aspects of snowshoeing, while many may be specific for a local area. Some of these are national or international. Below are a few organizations in the United States.

Appalachian Mountain Club
www.outdoors.org
This organization focuses on the northeastern United States. There are resources for hikers and snowshoers, with a lot of great trails and huts throughout New Hampshire.

Everytrail
www.everytrail.com
This great site contains free resources for finding trails.

Snowshoes.com
www.snowshoes.com
Here you will find information on events, learning to snowshoe, and locations of snowshoe trails, as well as a forum and news.

Snowshoe Magazine
www.snowshoemag.com
This site has interesting articles and photos about snowshoeing.

Trails.com

www.trails.com

This subscription site pulls many resources together to make finding information on a specific trail easy.

The United States Snowshoe Association

www.snowshoeracing.com

The association provides information on snowshoe racing and is a resource for snowshoe organizations.

Index

About the Author

Eli Burakian is a profes-
sional photographer who
lives in Vermont with his
exceedingly patient and
culinarily gifted wife, Julia.
Eli is currently employed
as the Dartmouth College
photographer in Hanover,
New Hampshire. His two
main passions of long-
distance backpacking and telemark skiing combine well with his love of
landscape photography. They combine only slightly less well with full-
time employment.

Eli is currently seeking a well-endowed mountain-loving patron
whose only goal in life is to see the natural world represented in
stunning detail in large fine art prints. In the meantime, he is working on
his skills as a rapper and hopes someday to become a photograpper
(seriously!).